Newell Dwight Hillis

How the inner light failed

Newell Dwight Hillis

How the inner light failed

ISBN/EAN: 9783741193064

Manufactured in Europe, USA, Canada, Australia, Japa

Cover: Foto ©ninafisch / pixelio.de

Manufactured and distributed by brebook publishing software
(www.brebook.com)

Newell Dwight Hillis

How the inner light failed

How the Inner Light Failed.

SAMSON is the Hercules or Othello of his age. He stands forth with the stern simplicity and majesty of a classical hero. In an era when law and government were unknown, and every man did that which was right in his own eyes, there appeared this gigantic fellow, who had the strength of Charlemagne and the patience of Ulysses. Disciplined from birth in the practice of temperance and sobriety, he grew up to a noble strength and a brawny beauty. Generous and lovable, he was also impetuous, abrupt and heedless. For men of force are generally men of faults; and this youth was one in whom feelings and impulses rose with the might of mountain freshets, that overflow their banks and devastate the wide-lying fields.

His career, full of strange adventure, reminds us of other heroes ancient and modern. Like Hercules, his sunny locks fell upon his brawny shoulders. Like Ulysses, his skill in strategy confounds his enemies. He rends ropes asunder like willow wands, and carries away the gates of the jail in which he had been imprisoned. Like King Arthur, he was betrayed by a woman's love. Like Hannibal, who drove the Roman herds into his camp to send them forth with fire brands tied upon their horns, that, rushing homeward, the animals might fire the harvest fields and destroy the ricks and barns to which they came, so Samson sent foxes with fire brands into the fields of standing grain to confuse his enemies. Nature crowned the youth with strength; at last strength crowned him king. Soon he brought the Philistines into subjection, and caused quiet once more to reign throughout the land.

But with ease came self-indulgence. His passions were fiends that lurked in ambush within his body. Once the tension of his moral nature was loosened he plunged into sin. Soon the giant threw himself into the arms of a beautiful woman. Delilah is Tennyson's Vivian, translated into terms of ancient life and thought. Charming him with her beauty, she plotted his overthrow. One night when his enemies lay secreted beyond the door Delilah, with wine, stole away Samson's strength and wisdom; then the lovely traitoress opened the doors, and his enemies

How the Inner Light Failed

leaped in to overpower the giant and put out his eyes. Striking swiftly and strongly, the rebels overcame Samson's soldiers and once more overran the land. Then for years, bereft, forlorn and blind, Samson toiled as a slave, grinding corn for the soldiers who kept his prison.

It is a piteous tragedy! The son had disappointed his parents, the general had betrayed his army, the ruler had enslaved his people, the giant had shorn away his own strength. The essence of the wretched story is that, sinning against his finer feelings, slowly the spiritual sense in the man had been destroyed until, in the pathetic words of the writer, it is said : "Samson wist not that God had departed from him." For an inner blindness went before and prefigured

How the Inner Light Failed

these outer sightless sockets. In his tragedy of "Samson Agonistes," Milton tells us Samson was blinder than his blindness, carried a weight heavier than his chains.

For men, great and small, victory hastens toward defeat when the inner light begins to fail. With nature and God one law is inexorable—he who disuses or misuses a faculty must lose it. One of the great singers of the day tells us that the neglect of exercise for the vocal cords for a single week means that flabby notes will creep into the tones. When Wallace, the scientist, was traveling over the deserted plains of the Euphrates he noticed that the wheat had reverted to the wild rice from which it was derived. It is said that in 1861, when the Northern army entered Virginia, the farmers fled from their homes to take

9

refuge in the city. Four years later, when they returned, the husbandmen found that their strawberries, once tame and large, had returned to the original type and become small and wild, while roses, once double and of every hue, had begun the reversion to the wild rose, always single and pink. In the animal world also the neglect of any faculty is fatal. When the traveler enters the Mammoth Cave he finds the subterranean lakes are filled with fish. At first glance the eyes of the fish seems perfect, but flashing his lantern before them, the scientist discovers the fish is blind. With his scalpel and microscope Drummond found that, while the front of the eye was perfect, behind there was only a mass of ruins. Disuse had turned the optic nerve into a dead, insensate, atrophied thread, along which vision had never flashed.

In every realm Nature withdraws her gift from him who neglects or misuses it. Neglecting vision, the mole is punished with blindness; neglecting wings, the flying-fish finds these members hanging feebly by its side; neglecting to use the sap it receives, the branch withers, rots and falls away from the tree; while that monk who made a vow not to lift his hand from his side for a period of years found at last his arm a withered, helpless thing— dead, yet hanging to a living body. For use is life, neglect is atrophy and death. There is no talent that comes unasked; there is no grace of mind and heart that stays un-urged. Happy, indeed, is he who hath ears to hear the still small voice that whispers, "He who neglects his finer spiritual sentiment shall

How the Inner Light Failed

find that the inner light hath failed."

This law of atrophy through disuse is also mental law and esthetic. Nature gives every person a fixed amount of energy of brain and body. If the youth decides to consume all his time and strength in making his arms big and his legs brawny, he ends his career a physical giant, indeed, but also an intellectual pigmy. Contrariwise, the student who secludes himself in a closet or cloister, despising his body, will become feeble in body in proportion as he is strong in brain. Abnormal development in one direction is absolutely prohibitive of normal growth in another.

In the history of his mental life Charles Darwin describes how the working of this law affected his character. In youth he was exceedingly fond of poetry and music. But

How the Inner Light Failed

early in his career he spent five years exploring the forests and rivers of South America and sailing through the islands of the Pacific. These years developed in him an intense desire to give his life to the pursuit of natural history. Through a full score of years he gave every moment of his time and every particle of his strength to the study of roots and seeds and flowers, of eggs and birds and beasts. At the age of fifty Darwin discovered that his love of music and poetry had faded away through disuse. The proportion of intellectual force that belonged to the taste and imagination had been given to the faculties of observation. Robbed of their food, the esthetic faculties had decayed and finally died.

In the hour of ill-health, when he needed the relaxation of song and drama, the great scientist wrote very pathetically: "If I had to live my life again I would have made a rule to read some poetry and listen to some music at least once every week; for perhaps the parts of my brain now atrophied would thus have been kept active through use. The loss of these tastes is a loss of happiness, and may possibly be injurious to the intellectual and more probably to the moral character, by enfeebling the emotional part of our nature." With greater sorrow does Mr. Darwin refer to the decline of his spiritual faculty. Through neglect he lost his religious sense, with the loss of his taste for poetry and music. Looking back to his youth, the aged scientist tells us that his original plan was to be a clergyman.

"Formerly," he writes, "I was

How the Inner Light Failed

led to the firm conviction of God
and of the immortality of the
soul. In my journal I wrote that
whilst standing in the midst of the
grandeur of the Brazilian forest, 'It
is not possible to give an adequate
idea of the higher feelings of won-
der, admiration and devotion which
fill and elevate the mind.' I well
remember my conviction that there
is more in man than the mere breath
of his body. But now the grandest
scene would not cause any such conviction and feelings to rise in my
mind. It may be truly said that I
am like a man who has become color-
blind; and the universal belief by
men of the existence of redness
makes my present loss of perception
of not the least value as evidence.
Disbelief crept over me at a very
slow rate, but was at last complete.
The rate was so slow that I felt no

distress." In his better hours, in-deed, the old embers sometimes flamed up. One day the Duke of Argyle said to him: "It is impossible to look upon such wonders as the fertilization of orchids without seeing that they are the effect and expression of mind." Mr. Darwin looked at the duke very hard and said: "Well, that often comes over me with overwhelming force, but at other times," and he shook his head vaguely, "it seems to go away."

Pathetic, indeed the story of the atrophy of the imagination and conscience. For those who have eyes to see, each poem or picture, each book or statue or speech is an open mirror in which is clearly revealed the very soul of Him who created it. Among the recent biographies is the

*Life and Letters of Darwin, Vol. I., page 316.

How the Inner Light Failed

story of the life and art of one who died a member of the Royal Academy. The author's love for his subject is plain, but at a certain point in the book the reader perceives that the artist has ceased to be the author's ideal hero. This glorious youth enters the scene like a strong man rejoicing to run a race. The sweet note of the skylark is in his voice. Great ideals shine in his eyes. The light never seen on land or sea pulsates and throbs in his pictures, as in the harvest fields the waves of air grow and pulsate with autumnal heat and color. But at a certain point in his career the artist took a step that was right before the law, but wrong, indeed, in the higher ideals. "Never again," says his biographer, "did he paint a great picture."

Not but that the painter still held

his position; it was not that men ceased to admire his portraits; all confessed that his flesh tints were bewitchingly beautiful; it was that a little mud showed in the eyes of each angel he painted; that an earthly tinge crept into the face of each seraph; that his own tones became metallic. The artist died full of honors, little dreaming, perhaps, that his supreme power died thirty years before with the death of his highest ideals. Like Samson, he wist not that the divine gift had passed from him forever.

In every other realm of art he who hath sinned against his better self hath lost his right to leadership. Here is Byron eagerly coveting a place among the immortals, yet accepting his clubfoot with cursings and bitterness; while Paul, accepting his thorn in the flesh with sweet-

ness, thereby was exalted and transfigured. The poet wishes to be a
hero for the public while privately
tasting the sweets of profligacy.
Sinning against his finer feelings,
his art steadily declined, his genius
was slowly eclipsed, until at thirty-
five years it passed into the sere and
yellow leaf. And thus, with all the
children of genius and inspiration,
neglect of a faculty or its abuse is
swiftly followed by ruin and loss.
Once an artist has chosen evil and
not good, his clay model ceases to be
art and becomes only a mass of mud;
his music loses its sweetness and
becomes a mere strumming of keys;
his eloquence loses its moral purpose
and becomes a jingle of beautiful
phrases; his manhood loses its character and he stands forth only a
bundle of flesh, an animated biped
to be kept warm by soft wool, to be

fed upon stalled ox, but of whom it must be said, as of Samson, "This man wist not that God had departed from him nor knew that the inner light had failed."

The faculty that crowns man king is conscience, and all the great dramatists have believed that conscience may be killed. The atrophy of the finer feelings is a thought that seems to have fascinated great men. Shakespeare and Goethe, Jean Paul and Victor Hugo, Hawthorne and Dickens, all these have made a study of the soul's descent toward demonhood. Each author has caused some youth to enter the scene crowned with glorious strength, beauty and purity, and then, through self-indulgence and sin, slowly he paralyzes his sense of right until remorse becomes literally a lost art.

In his study of Donatello, Haw-

thorne invents a legend that inter-
prets his thought of a mutilated
conscience.   In the olden time there
lived a knight who loved a beautiful
maiden, either woman or sprite, who
dwelt in a fountain hidden away in
a deep forest.   She was as young as
a May morning, and her presence
was sunshine in the boy's soul. She
taught the youth how to make
friends with the crickets and squir-
rels and how to call the thrush and
the robin to eat from his hand.   In
his merriest hours she gladdened
his humor, and in his darkest moods,
with a swift touch she charmed the
fret and fever quite away.   At last
the youth journeyed for a short time
to a distant city. There he fell into
evil paths and on a fatal day sinned
a great sin.

When a week had passed, the
knight one morning appeared again

How the Inner Light Failed

in the forest. With bloodshot eyes and stumbling steps he hastened along the pathway to the fountain. Strangely enough he seemed afraid and ever cast furtive glances all about the woods. Suddenly he stopped and whistled to his forest friends. Soon the whirr of wings was in the air, and the stealthy flutter of the forest children was heard among the leaves. But all at once, whatever the reason, there were a rush and a scamper of little feet and the frightened cries of fleeing birds. Then, with a wild cry, the boy hastened on and threw himself down beside the fountain, only to find the water shrinking away before his lips and leaving his fevered face uncooled. Nor did the maiden give answer to his call, though there seemed to come a cry of bitter woe. Only once did he behold

How the Inner Light Failed

that blessed face, and then it was lying upon the waters with a bloody stain upon the forehead, for the knight's sin had slain the fountain girl. In that dark hour the bow of hope faded from the sky, the green sod ceased to be elastic to his feet, the sky was leaden to his looks, the sun itself became a patch of darkness, and conscience and God became a jargon of words.

What does the author mean by the legend? It is the story of Donatello, who hath sinned against himself. It is George Eliot's Tito, whose sin has ceased to cut a bloody gash in conscience. It is Jean Paul's Charles, who made himself a demon and lost all power of feeling remorse. It is Macbeth, who hath slain happiness and murdered sleep. It is Samson, who hath injured the mind's eye until the light hath

failed. It is Judas, who hath betrayed his Master and played the
traitor to his own soul. It is the
epic of man's soul, and the story of
one in whom the inner light hath
failed.

Mr. Darwin's statement that he
had dwarfed his imagination and his
religious faculty to the extent that
his opinion regarding musical and
moral problems was as worthless as
though he were color-blind, suggests
an analysis of the causes of religious atrophy. Like the faculty of
reason, of judgment, or of memory,
the religious sense becomes strong
through culture and exercise, or
weak through neglect and want of
nourishment. Much of what is
called modern doubt and the decay
of faith is simply the result of pre-
occupation and the neglect of the
finer feelings and faculties. In our

How the Inner Light Failed

day competition is fierce, the pace of life is fast, and the temptation is to throw the whole being into business. Soul-culture, through meditation and quiet reflection, is almost a lost art. Men's minds are so filled with trade and commerce as to preclude the culture of conscience and hope with faith and love.

A recent poem sends a hard-worked physician, a teacher and a scientist upon a holiday to the country. Returning, the physician brings back a series of observations as to the effect of early hours, excessive toil, and improper food upon the health of the rural population; the teacher returns with a note-book filled with improper idioms and local phrases peculiar to mountaineers, while the scientist is happy in that he has found ten new kinds of bugs. Each man had eyes for his own realm, but was blind to every other.

In England the leisure-classes understand well the principles of culture through reflection and worship. The most important contribution made to religious literature during the past year was "Foundations of Belief," written by Mr. Balfour, a leader in the House of Commons. This man, who is the First Lord of the Treasury, never reads a newspaper, substituting books and magazines instead.

Through sixty years Mr. Gladstone entered the nearest chapel or church every morning at nine o'clock for his morning prayers, and for sixty years he kept Sunday for the culture of his religious nature, scrupulously precluding all thoughts of politics or statecraft. To this habit he ascribed his health and intellectual fertility.

But the hygienics of the spiritual and the mental nature seem almost unknown in our land. Our politicians are politicians and nothing more; our lawyers and physicians are seldom authors; also in the realm of literature, of poetry and of religion. Our people have forgotten that Sunday is the soul's brooding day, and that worship, song and prayer cleanse away the grime of life, sharpen the intellectual faculties, enable the soul to take its observations and lay out the voyage toward the distant harbor.

It is said the great men of New England, dying, have left no successors, and this is true largely because of the waxing of materialism and the waning of religious faculty.

How the Inner Light Failed

Nor can there ever be another great literary or artistic epoch for our country until the common people have learned again the art of brooding, of soul-worship and aspiration. For great men are simply the voices for a great generation. Popular intelligence and the diffused religious life are simply the atmosphere in which the high talent of our orator, or artist, or dramatist, or philosopher is to find his nourishment and stimulation. Great men stand upon the shoulders of the common people. The problem of our day is the problem of the revival of the spiritual faculty in order to the bringing in of a great outburst in the higher life and arts. Doubtless knowledge is more widely diffused than ever before; but it is equally certain that the lack of care and training of the imagination and the higher religious sentiments has resulted in a distinct loss in our mental grip, as is evinced in our journals, our politics, our life, our literature. This is a generation in which parents are permitting their children to grow up as moral and religious weaklings. The theory of millions of parents is, "Let the child wait until he has grown and then choose his own religion." More than two generations ago an English statesman uttered this sentiment in the presence of Coleridge. Leading his friend into the garden, Coleridge said: "I have decided not to put out any vegetables this spring, but to wait until August and let the garden decide for itself whether it prefers weeds or strawberries."

The Japanese have studied the art of dwarfing trees. Often a little

How the Inner Light Failed

pot scarcely four inches in diameter contains a pine tree only twelve inches high but one hundred years old. The tendency of modern life, also, is to make men spiritual dwarfs, so that multitudes who are physically matured remain children in the spiritual realm. Many feel keenly the sorrow of physical inferiority who never seem to realize that conscience and their moral sentiments are dwarfed and wrapped up in grave-clothes, so that, dying, they carry into that other realm a multitude of moral deformities and spiritual abnormalities.

We need not be surprised, therefore, that he who has dulled his heart with avarice or cruelty; he who has wasted his power in folly or iniquity; he who has debased himself by some great evil, is out of touch with the sweetest sights in nature, hears not the sweetest sounds, discerns not God's footsteps in his daily life. When Shakespeare declared that the man who has no music in his soul is fit for treacheries, he tells us that there is something wrong in a man who has lost the vision of the unseen and the sight of the invisible. The pure in heart see God, while the unjust, the iniquitous, the oppressors of the poor will not believe in Him. One might as well expect a savage to appreciate the frescoes of Raphael, or a Hottentot to understand the dramas of Shakespeare.

To all young hearts standing upon life's threshold, whose feet will soon stand within the greatest century that has ever passed over our earth, there comes the reflection that victory and happiness move swiftly toward sorrow and defeat for him in whom the inner light hath failed. For the saddest sight on earth is not that of a youth stricken down and laid beneath the turf just at the moment when others enter upon their career—earth's greatest tragedy is the tragedy of those who have fallen from integrity and virtue, as stars fall out of the sky. A ship may lose its sails and rudder, but if it retain its compass it may yet reach the harbor. But in life all is lost when man loses conscience. That rock is fatal to nobility.

The mountaineers of Tennessee tell that when the wild pigeons are flying southward the leaders of the long column will swerve from the course to avoid some danger, and thenceforth all the column following after will make that same wide turn. Trappers have found that when a beaver has been caught in a trap

How the Inner Light Failed

the next animal finds some odor clinging to the steel jaws that speaks of the suffering of its fellow, so that trappers use fragrant oils to deceive the cautious creatures. Strange that animals should be wiser than men! Surely it ought to be enough that one noble youth suffered the atrophy of his religious faculty. Yet the old traps still avail for man's enthrallment, and thirty pieces of silver, a wedge of gold, a purple robe, a bewitching Delilah, a tinsel ornament, still avail for man's overthrow.

For the children of wisdom there comes the reflection that happiness and the sense of victory are only for those who live for conscience and duty and the soul's higher ideals. Olive Shreiner has a dream of a mother who prays beside the cradle

and broods lovingly above her babe.
While she prayed she dreamed and
saw messengers drawing near to
proffer strange gifts. One said, "I
am Health, and whom I touch shall
never know pain nor sickness." Another said, "I am Wealth, and whom
I touch shall know neither poverty
nor want." Another said, "I am
Fame, and at my touch the child
shall rise to a place beside the immortals." Another said, "I am love,
and at my touch in the darkest hour
a friendly hand shall be out-
stretched." Last of all came one
with furrowed face and hollow
cheeks and burning eyes, who offered
not health nor wealth nor fame
nor love, but only this: that he
could cause the child to love his ideals
and never lose them. "This is my
gift," said he. "His ideals shall be
real to him." And then the mother,

kneeling down, clasped the garments of that messenger and cried out, "Touch, oh, touch my child!"

For all who thirst for the old, deep, sweet feelings of childhood and youth, even as David thirsted for a drink of water from his father's well at Bethlehem, there comes this thought: that, under the tender touch of God, the hearts of men grown old and gray in a life of temptation and sin may become again as the heart of a little child. For man there is a great truth in this: that Milton in his vision, saw Samson upon the last day of his life, blind, indeed, and grinding corn in the prison of his enemies, yet lifting his sightless eyes in penitence and prayer toward God, until the solar light flooded his face and filled his heart with happiness, and in his death brought him victory again

How the Inner Light Failed

over ease and selfishness and sin. It is Milton's evangel of hope to this generation, with its sorrow and sin, that there is a Saviour divine, the Christ, whose sacred touch heals the broken-hearted, opens the door for the endungeoned and recovers sight to the blind.

How the Inner Light Grows.

" Evening and morning and noon will
I pray........"—Psalm lv., 17..

How the Inner Light Grows.

WHEN the peerage book of earth's kings is finally made up, the pages will include the name of this minstrel shepherd boy, who passed quickly from sheepcote to king's palace, and took his place among the immortals. The strangely checkered career of this chivalrous youth reminds us of Scotland's hero, Robert Bruce, and also of Robert Burns, the people's poet. Gifted with a strangely rich and lovable nature, this shepherd minstrel moved among men with that irresistible fascination only the greatest possess. He enters the scene the child of innocence and all sweet song. Soon, aided by his flute, he sang his way into the king's heart, and, like a sunbeam, passed into the gloomy palace. When a few months had gone by the boy was the champion of the army, the idol of the people, the dearest friend of Jonathan, and then, with a single leap, he bounded in to the throne itself. By reason of his self-reliance and prudence, his boldness of attack and his courage in defense, David has been called the greatest of the Jewish kings. But now that long time hath passed, we all do see that he has his fame, not because he was a king and a born leader of men, but because he was a poet, and sang of human life with all its pathos and mystery. Centuries ago his granite crumbled and his marble became dust, but his sweet psalms and songs do still abide.

To Robert Burns came the daisy,

the field-mouse, and the poor cotter,
to be baptized with beauty; to
David, the shepherd boy, came the
withering grass, the fading flowers,
the shepherd and his flock, the dis-
solving clouds, the abiding mount-
ains, to be blessed with the immortality of sweet song. Immeasur-
able the debt that civilization owes
to this youth, whose songs have
consoled man's sorrows, refined his
griefs and exalted his aspirations.
Be the reasons what they may, the
influence of generals, statesmen and
inventors is less deep and abiding
than the influence of those poets
who have sung of love and grief,
of war and worship, and of the shep-
herd-care of God.

It was a poet who led the Greek
barbarians toward arts and indus-
tries. It was a poet who marshaled
the Roman hosts for victory. It

was a poet who ushered in the Renaissance and the new Italy. To the sound of music our soldiers marched away to battle, and sweet song made their strong right arms invincible. It may be true, as Curtis said, that not "until we know why the rose is red, the dewdrop pure, or the rainbow beautiful," can we know why the poet is the best benefactor of humanity, but certain it is he is the harmonizer, strengthener and consoler of society. The generations journey forward following the leadership of those who sing of liberty and love, of joy and grief, and death. Happy this shepherd-poet to whom it was given to write the songs with which the mother soothed her child, with which the hero inspired his hosts.

Clothed, then, with the full force of genius, with the eternal melodies

How the Inner Light Grows

murmuring upon his lips, what has this child of inspiration to do with stated hours for prayer, with iron rules for psalm and song? Is not regularity the antithesis of inspiration? Is not rigidity the death of poetic ardor? Will not rule and habit make the soul to move along a dusty road? Spontaneity is the prerogative of poets, as are also a certain dewy freshness of thought, and a untrammeledness of feeling and fancy. Surely the poet has the right to break down all fences and bars and wander forth, free and careless as a bird or bounding fawn. What has the poet who sings the songs of the ages to do with "dry-as-dust" rules, with the systematic piety that prays at six o'clock, at twelve o'clock, and again when the evening shadows fall? Yet these songs, that have the freshness of

How the Inner Light Grows

the new-blown rose, blossomed from a heart that was rooted in regularity, cultivated by stated meditations, with its songs and prayers ordered by system and method. Go where the poet would—standing at dawn upon the grass to meet with adoring thoughts the gaze of the vaulted sky, musing at noon amidst the crowded market-place or going forth at twilight to behold an unseen hand drape the clouds and poise the clustering stars— always for him the hilltop or the arbor, the field or the forest, were sanctuaries, and this hour or that was good enough for rapturous prayer and song. Let mediocre people order their religion by rule, let dull and stupid folk control their higher spiritual life by system, but let this poet be freed from all trammeling laws, and pray or not, as his mood may be. Yet, swift comes David's sharp rebuke: "Evening and morning and noon will I pray." For the poet it is system that deepens the tides of inspiration, and method that nourishes the forces of feeling and moral sentiment. At dawn, therefore, David's heart rose with the rising sun; at noon his aspirations ascended like the clouds of incense rising above the temple he had built; at eventide his thoughts became golden chariots in which his soul rode upward to meet its God.

The sanction of genius and the sympathy of earth's greatest minds and hearts are ours, therefore, when we plead for systematic religion, for method and rule in ordering the higher life of the spirit. The age, the generation that represents the apotheosis of mediocrity may be for-

given for making haste to cast off
what it calls the trammels of religion, and the irksomeness of rules
and laws. But surely the era of in-
tellect should understand that system feeds inspiration, that method
is the sign of power and greatness.
Uninteresting, indeed, the dry husk,
the sere leaf, the withered stalk of
corn, the shriveled mummy; but full
of interest and fascination the new-
blown flower, the moist bunch of
figs, the sweet face of a babe.

Homer spake of the "rosy fin-
gers" and the "dewy cheeks of
dawn." Long afterward Emerson
wrote: "I am cheered by the moist,
warm, budding, melodious morning." The two poets were sepa-
rated by 2,500 years, yet the
morning was still new and glowing because nature still worked by
rule, the sun in its rising never be-

How the Inner Light Grows

ing a stroke of the clock behind, nor
a stroke late in its setting. By rule
also coal dust crystallizes into the
diamond and the clay into the sap-
phire; by rule nature paints the
violet and lays the warm tones into
apple or peach. By rule April
wreathes her orchards with pink and
frail-floretted snow. By rule August
covers the hills with the golden glow
of clustering food. By rule Septem-
ber makes the valley, covered with
corn, to laugh and sing. Marveling
at the bounty of beauty that lay
upon the cheek of the babe, Wordsworth said: "The soul comes trail-
ing clouds of glory." Now this
blush of beauty upon the cheek without represents regular habits for
the health within.

Contrariwise, the lack of regularity in eating or sleeping will drive
the bloom from the cheek, cause

black circles under the eyes, a furry
coat upon the tongue, and take
from the brain the fine edge of its
thinking. Nature has her beauty
through the emphasis of that system and method which the poet
indicates are the source of his inspiration and ardor. For life means
system and order; death means con-
fusion and chaos. The toadstool,
that is irregular in its time and
method of growth, and the apples of
Sodom, stuffed with soot and ashes,
represent the disregard of systematic growth. The harvests are, indeed, "the lyric thoughts of God,
falling from his Almighty solitude,"
yet they fall at stated periods. The
seasons are the notes flying forth
from the strings of Nature's lyre
as "God's solemn hands wander
over the possibilities of beauty,"
yet these notes have their or-

How the Inner Light Grows

dained intervals. David's prayer
and song, rising at morning and
noon and evening, do but repeat
great Nature's plan and method.

If in Nature's realm system has
perfected our flowers and fruits, the
history of great writers tells us that
in the realm of literature systematic
toil has polished our most perfect
poems and perfected all great phi-
losophies. The artist-pupil looks
up to his master, the young musician
to his teacher; nevertheless, drudg-
ery hath gifts to bestow beyond the
wealth of famous instructors. Were
we to search out the secret of earth's
most eminent writers, we would
find that these votaries have, like
David, lingered morning, noon and
night in the temple of art, of eloquence or of sweet song. When Carlyle turned from his outlook upon
the career of great writers, he said

that the most enduring work in literature represents not the inspiration of genius, but the fruitage of systematic toil. He writes: "Neither Virgil nor Tacitus were ready writers. Shakespeare, we may fancy, wrote with rapidity, but not till he had thought with intensity; no easy writer he. Neither was Milton one of the mob of gentlemen who wrote with readiness."

Goethe tells us he had nothing sent to him in his sleep. Schiller never could conclude. Dante sees himself growing lean with his "Divine Comedy." The past year also has furnished a striking illustration of the fact that literature is the hardest of the trades. For the first time in the present century, perhaps, English literature has been without a single living novelist of world-wide reputation. But the jubilee

How the Inner Light Grows

poem of Rudyard Kipling has led all scholars to believe that a new and unrivaled force has entered the world of poetry and fiction. In originality, versatility and the sheer weight of mentality, this new author stands forth a striking figure; and there is no second. But by as much as Kipling surpasses other poets and novelists in originality, by so much does he surpass them in methodical industry. His genius is harnessed to system, his talent is regulated by rule. When the clock strikes the hour, his mind begins to work. His highest creative moods are controlled by habit and method. No fevered, fitful toil is his; no waiting for the wings of inspiration to fill his pages. At fixed times he toils and fulfills his noble task. Recently the drawing-rooms of London tried to lionize the gifted author. Lest

society, with its late hours, should
keep him from his desk when the
morning clock struck eight, Kipling
disappeared as suddenly and completely as if the earth had opened
and swallowed him up. For weeks
no man knew where telegram or let-
ter or book or newspaper would
reach him. At one altar he knelt—
the altar of System and Method; one
muse he worshiped—Industry. In
silence and obscurity he labored until his book was completed. Then he
came forth, pale and worn and well-
nigh paralyzed by that entire con·
centration of his being that gives
the peculiar quality to his work.
Like David, he found in the routine
of industry the hidings of his power.

Nor is Kipling a solitary exception.
When Hall Caine was questioned
regarding his £10,000 received for
"The Christian," he replied that

How the Inner Light Grows

the book represented several years of unremitting labor; that the notes made in the study of his characters would fill a barrel, and that three times the book was entirely rewritten. Plainly these modern candidates for fame are imitating Scott, whom Lockhart saw seated at his window writing page after page of manuscript all day long, until the candles were brought in, and far into the night. "King over all the novelists—Scott!" exclaimed Carlyle. So regularly did Scott work that, when his publishing house failed, Constable thought Scott's name was one to conjure with, and, going up to London, went to the Bank of England and asked the loan of £100,000, offering as security the splendid genius of his partner, Walter Scott, counting as good collateral this creative mind, because it was as regular as the rising sun, as certain as a quarry of marble or a mine of gold.

But, it is said, one realm there is in which inspiration is everything, routine and rule nothing. In eloquence and art, it is affirmed, man must wait the coming of his nobler moods; that the greatest artists are born, not trained; that the highest eloquence represents certain critical and unexpected moments that of necessity can neither be anticipated nor prepared for. Fortunately the history of our orators is not hidden. For, next to tales of adventure and heroism, men love stories of eloquence. Full and fascinating is Edward Everett's story of Daniel Webster in his exalted mental moods, when he stood forth with Jovelike front, his bronze complexion glowing as with inward fire, his

eyes blazing lightning, represent-
ing, as did scarce any other man of
his time, a true conception of what
a magnificent human being God's
creative hand can produce! Yet no
man has ever lived whose eloquence
was more truly the fruitage of culture and training from vocal effects,
and posture and gesture down to
the very buttons upon his coat, than
was that eloquence of Daniel Webster.

History tells of no orator nor
statesman whose supremest gifts
have not represented systematic
practice. In his youth, five times
aloud did Pitt translate the orations
of Demosthenes, until, by drill, he
made it possible to do his best thinking upon his feet. An English author speaks of Mr. Beecher's "Orations for Freedom," with its five
chapters, delivered in as many cities

of England, as "the greatest single political speech of our century." His eloquence was something to dream about. His voice was as sweet as a lute and as loud as a trumpet. When he rose to impassioned sublimity men said it "thundered." Yet Paganini himself, practicing for seven hours each day, never gave himself up more completely to incessant drill than did Mr. Beecher during that period when he was preparing for his public career. Every day, during three years, he tells us, he went into a forest and spent from two to three hours in exploding the vowels and consonants and developing his voice in its lowest register. Literally might he have said: "Evening and morning and noon do I lift up my voice." At length, through systematic practice, the orator stood forth a born king over men, to call down summer or winter upon the multitude, to stretch forth his hand like a scepter or to beckon man with sweet persuasion. Practice lent the youth power, and power made him king.

Since system and method have done much for literature, art and eloquence, we seem justified in assuming that it bears relation to the culture of moral sentiments. Nothing is risked in affirming that our generation needs something to bring back the freshness and joy, the bloom and beauty of life. For some reason the soul now has dust upon its wings. The din of the street, the roar and rattle of wagons, have drowned out the still small voice of God. Jaded, weary and disgusted, men run fussily about, sickened with life's excitements, yet ever seeking new pleasure◦

How the Inner Light Grows

Multitudes are overwrought and incapable of nobler joys. Meditation is a lost art. Action now is glorified. Society looks suspiciously upon solitude, and the poet or seer or student who prays at evening and morning and noon is thought to be guilty of a foolish waste of time. When the young traveler, who was also a hero-worshiper, asked the Scotch farmer the way to Carlyle's house, the man replied: " Thomas Carlyle, poor, foolish, good-for-nothing fellow, is not here, but James is. Ah, James is a good man ! He drives more swine to Ecclefechan market than any other man in the country." The modern hero is the man who, in a single year, has manufactured a hundred thousand coats or five million hose.

Society is in danger of forgetting he men who have never entered the

How the Inner Light Grows

"madding crowd," and who, in silence and solitude, have done their work; for all the publicity of modern commerce begins with the privacy of some scholar. The man of commerce and affairs often looks down upon some Emerson, living for thirty years in solitude, in the morning brooding over his books, in the afternoon walking through the fields with notebook in hand. For years the English shopkeepers spoke contemptuously of Darwin, who built no barn, reaped no harvest, made no fortune; who for twenty years never once appeared in the world of politics or trade or commerce, but evening and morning and noon watched the buds and leaves unroll; noted the development of the earthworm, analyzed flowers, butterflies and birds. Yet that simple, meditative man gave a new impulse to

commerce and to his age, and developed within his generation a
power to invent tools and instruments that have made Darwin to be
the indirect creator of as much
material wealth, perhaps, as any
merchant or manufacturer of his
generation. The market-place and
the factory owe much to thinkers,
just as the branches bowing down
with ripe fruit owe much to the
roots working in silence and darkness. For material riches without,
oegin with meditation and the en-
richment and culture of the soil
within.

Send some young Wordsworth
into solitude, bidding him brood
evening and morning and noon upon
the hills, and he will write great
poems. Send some Turner into
fields and forests to study lights
and shades of nature, and bid him

brood in silence for five and forty years, and the day will come when he will leave the nation six and twenty thousand noble pictures and sketches. Let Moses go into the desert, there to brood for forty years, and he will write the laws of justice upon which all codes and institutions still do rest. Send that Egyptian boy out into the desert as a hermit, and brooding alone beneath the stars of the unseen God who dwells above them, he will found the science of astronomy. Let Linnæus dwell alone in icy Lapland, midst scenes poor in vegetation, and in solitude he will write his name high among those botanists who have lived midst tropic vegetation. Send John forth to his solitary Patmos, and there, where earth's images are dimmed, the vision of the Eternal City will grow bright.

How the Inner Light Grows

Lingering alone upon the mountain tops, Christ saw the heavens open and was himself transfigured. Thus each Tauler and Fénélon, Newton and Keble, each hero and saint of the spiritual life has said with David: "Evening and morning and noon do I pray."

No plea for systematic religion is complete that does not emphasize the influence of method in worship. Our fathers and the heroes of yesterday loved the Sunday as the heart loves the murmuring brooks. Young Niebuhr, hastening from Rome, climbed the Alps and looked out toward his beloved Italy. Not otherwise have the great minds of all ages looked upon Sunday as a noble mountain peak upon which they climbed to behold their world. Speaking not as a moralist, but as a statesman, Washington, at the beginning of the Revolution, issued an order beginning: "That the troops may have an opportunity of attending public worship as well as to take some rest, the General in future excuses them from fatigue duty on Sunday. We can have but little hope of the blessing of heaven on our arms if we insult it by our impiety and folly." Webster also discerned that worship stands in vital relation to our institutions. In his great argument he urged that Sunday was a law of nature as well as of God, and that no individual or nation habitually disregarding it had failed to fall upon disaster and grief. Emerson is equally explicit: "Christianity has given us the Sabbath, the jubilee of the whole world, whose light brings welcome alike into the closet of the philosopher, into the garret of toil, and

into the prison cells, and everywhere
suggests, even to the vile, the dig-
nity of spiritual being."

Because Sunday is the soul's par-
lor day, the day for reason and imagination and conscience, our age,
with its overwrought bodies, its
overtaxed brains, its jaded hearts,
needs the day as our fathers did
not. Unfortunately, former generations emphasized long prayers, long
sermons, long faces, built prison
walls around the Sabbath, made the
day bondage, made the worship tyr-
anny. Now, in the reaction, care-
lessness is developing lawlessness.
Many fear lest the day is becoming
a day of the body, dedicated to open-
air games and exercises. It is coming to stand for perspiration,
not inspiration. Formerly Sunday
furnished the spiritual force that
wrote books, painted pictures,

refined homes and communities.
Now it furnishes work for laundries.
Recently 20,000 people entered
the gates of a race-course during
a single Sunday afternoon. One
Sunday morning during the past
summer a kindergartner noticed a
young girl leading some thirty little
children into a park. Inquiry developed the fact that the mothers
and fathers had gone forth for an
all-day's bicycle tour into the country. Multitudes of young men and
women, confined in the foul store-
rooms and offices through six days
of the week, feel that no choice is
left them save to use Sunday for
recreation, even though the soul
does sit in its dungeon and starve.
Already the records of crime and
arrest upon Sunday are double
those of any other day of the week.

When Robert Collyer began his

ministry in New York he made a plea for worship and Sunday. Some there are, he said, who try to be their own temple and their own priest, worshiping God in the woods or meadows, instead of in the sanctuary. "What," he asks, "do you really do on the waters and in the woods and in your own homes, and what does it all come to? The drift of it all is to slay faith and to touch with paralysis the nerve of any grand endeavor. Few and far between are those who can live without worship. This 'own temple' and 'own priest' business is merely seeming, and the dumb things that run and fly worship God more truly than they do. There is one God of such things, and his name is the one they got from their godfathers and godmothers; one supreme service, and you spell it with four letters—

s-e-l-f; one grand purpose here, and that is to look after first person singular, and one thing to which they look forward when they get to the end, and that is—a leap in the dark."

President Hopkins told the students in Williams college that when they stopped kneeling in prayer they would soon stop praying in spirit. Thus, when the multitudes cease to flow into the sanctuary to bathe themselves in God's divine ether, to wash the grime from the soul's garments, to sharpen the dulled instruments of the spirit, that moment the bloom and beauty will begin to pass from our arts, our literature, our music, our laws, and the very springs of civilization will dry up.

Every Sunday, with a regularity that never is broken, our philosophers need to find their way into the sanctuary, that they may understand what Plato meant when he said: "Out of pity for the wretched life of mortals God set apart days of festal refreshment." Our statesmen need the Sabbath worship that they may put justice into laws and ethics into politics and love into service. Our young men and maidens need the hour of meditation, that, pondering upon the ways of God to men, they may find out the pathway God hath appointed for their young feet and be ordained for noble service. The poor, toiling in mines and forests, midst the rattle of machinery and the dust of factory, who for six days seem like captive and fettered eagles, need this day for remembering that the earth is not a huge barn; that its fruits are not fodder; that man is not a beast. No hour is more

precious for the reason that writes
books, the talent that paints pictures, the conscience that enacts
laws, than the hour dedicated to
worship, the place named the sanctuary, the day dedicated to God. As
the flowers and fruits do not come
to full perfection until they exhale
their sweetest perfume, so the soul
finds not its loftiest moods until it
rises through the pathless air, ex-
haling hope and love and aspiration
toward the unseen God.

David, at stated hours, kneeling
to lisp or sing his prayer; Job, ex-
panding his worship into noble
poems; Newton, praying beneath the
overhanging stars; Christ, making
it his custom to enter the syna-
gogue upon the Sabbath, to kneel
in worship—all tell us that the soul
is in its highest mood when it enters
into silence or into the sanctuary,

and, through adoring worship, strengthens that golden cord that binds it to the throne of love.

A traveler tells us that amidst the Arabian hills is a valley given up to the culture of odorous shrubs and spices, where the air is redolent of fragrance. Going away the visitor finds that the perfume clings to hair and garments for days.

Saddened by life's sordidness, depressed by the avarice, cunning, and cruelty of the street, the soul needs its hours of revery and worship, for rising into the purer, sweeter air where tranquility dwells. There, walking, musing, praying, ardor will return to the jaded sense. The heart again will burn, the fret and fever pass away, and the soul go forth, with David's freshness and ardor, indeed, and also with enduring strength from the Eternal God.